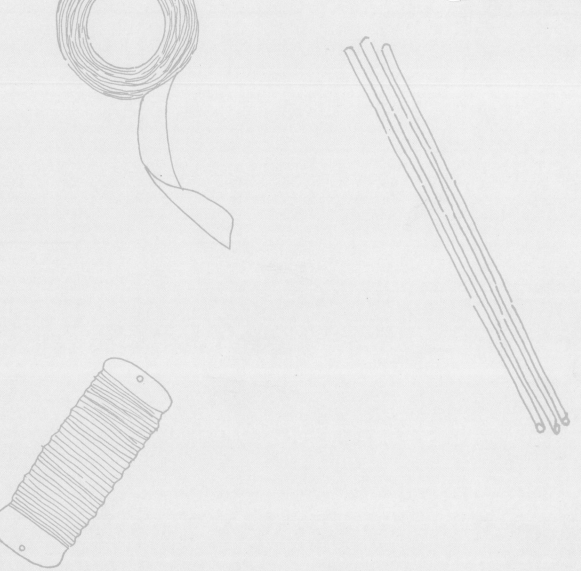

W9-DAQ-523

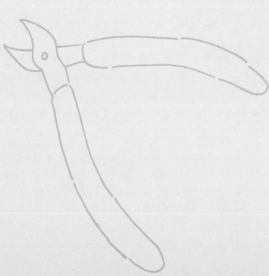

Floral Crafts
for the first time®

Floral Crafts
for the first time®

Ruby Begonia

Sterling Publishing Co., Inc.
New York
A Sterling/Chapelle Book

Chapelle, Ltd.
Owner: Jo Packham

Editor: Karmen Quinney

Staff: Areta Bingham, Kass Burchett, Ray Cornia, Jill Dahlberg, Marilyn Goff, Holly Hollingsworth, Susan Jorgensen, Barbara Milburn, Cindy Stoeckl, Kim Taylor, Sara Toliver, Desirée Wybrow

Technical Advisor: Ryan A. Smith

Photography: Kevin Dilley for Hazen Photography

The written instructions, designs, illustrations, photographs, and projects in this volume are intended for the personal use of the reader and may be reproduced for that purpose only. Any other use, especially commercial use, is forbidden under law without the written permission of the copyright holder.

Every effort has been made to ensure that all of the information in this book is accurate. However, due to differing conditions, tools, and individual skills, the publisher cannot be responsible for any injuries, losses, and/or any other damages which may result from the use of the information in this book.

If you have any questions or comments, please contact:

Chapelle, Ltd., Inc.
P.O. Box 9252
Ogden, UT 84409
Phone: (801) 621-2777
FAX: (801) 621-2788
e-mail: chapelle@chapelleltd.com
website: www.chapelleltd.com

Library of Congress Cataloging-in-Publication Data

10 9 8 7 6 5 4 3 2 1

A Sterling/Chapelle Book

Published by Sterling Publishing Co., Inc.
387 Park Avenue South, New York, NY 10016
© 2002 by Chapelle Limited
Distributed in Canada by Sterling Publishing
⅜ Canadian Manda Group, One Atlantic Avenue, Suite 105
Toronto, Ontario, Canada M6K 3E7
Distributed in Great Britain and Europe by Cassell PLC
Wellington House, 125 Strand, London WC2R 0BB, England
Distributed in Australia by Capricorn Link (Australia) Pty. Ltd.
P.O. Box 704, Windsor, NSW 2756, Australia
Printed in China
All Rights Reserved

Sterling ISBN 0-8069-7311-0

Ruby & Begonia

AN EMBARRASSMENT OF RICHES

204 Historic 25th Street
Ogden, Utah 84401
Phone 801.334.7829

WWW.RUBYANDBEGONIA.COM

Ruby & Begonia is not just another gift and decorative life-style store—it is the best of everything for you and your home. It is a destination for you to come and wrap yourself in a small but necessary luxury, surrender to a guilty pleasure, and discover your creative soul. In unique surroundings that change with each new month, Ruby & Begonia offers distinctive and one-of-a-kind items, some of which are vintage, while others are hand-crafted by the country's finest artisans. All are unique, extraordinary, and appeal to the buyer, to the giver, or to the recipient—each in a different and a personal way.

Ruby & Begonia is a newly established emporium whose approach to re-tailing is as innovative as the clients, who frequent it. It is the kind of place, where visitors travel from far and near to enjoy the displays that change with each new month; the decorating ideas that are simple, creative, and inexpen-sive; and the gift-giving suggestions that are perfect for a special someone.

Table of Contents

Floral Crafts for the first time

Introduction

Flowers in almost any form are more than just a source of beauty, they are a way of expressing an infinite variety of sentiments. They brighten a room, give it color, and naturally become one of its main decorative assets. Flowers can say everything or nothing at all. They symbolize a declaration of love, act as a sincere apology, or offer heartfelt condolences. Because flowers mean so many different things to so many, we plant them in our gardens, bring them indoors, and dry them to preserve their beauty. Or, sometimes when fresh flowers are unavailable, we use silk and paper flowers to imitate their natural beauty so that we are never without them.

Flowers have been an integral part of everyday life as well as its celebrated special occasions for centuries. Traditionally, because flowers grew in a natural state and were untouched by science, the popular arrangement styles of the past were determined by flower availability, fashion, and the interior design trends of the day. Today, however, flowers are selected and arranged almost without limitations or restrictions due to modern science's ability to breed flowers to withstand certain weather conditions, live longer, grow smaller or larger in size, and show new colors and color combinations.

The Romans used lavish floral arrangements to decorate their residences and meeting places. In medieval times, flowers were grown in private gardens and believed to have had special properties that warded off disease and infection. The seventeenth- and eighteenth-century floral arrangements boasted bold color and flower-type combinations squeezed into lovely classic vases. Flowers were adored in the Victorian era, especially the rose. New varieties of roses were bred, and the floral arrangements incorporated fashion accessories of the day, such as lace, beads, and velvety ribbons.

A more natural approach to floral arranging emerged in the 1930s and 1940s, and wild and nursery-grown floral arrangements took on gentler shapes. Floral arrangements of the 1950s toyed with gaudy, bright color combinations, and containers that mismatched in a carefree spirit. Daring color combinations remained popular in the following decade, and a favorite arrangement style was the "unordered" look, where the final product appeared effortless and natural. Today, as was true in the 1970s, pretty much anything goes.

Look around at the world you live in and create your art with flowers as a reflection. Color schemes, shapes, and textures that are part of your life can be echoed in your floral arrangement. A garden of perennials, a parkway framed in wildflowers, a corner flower stand, and a centerpiece at either a five-star hotel or a tiny out-of-the-way bed and breakfast are examples of arrangement idea sources. Inspiration can also come from the upholstery on a living-room love seat, the patterns in an autumn tablecloth, an exquisite eighteenth-century painting, or any cherished memento or object of beauty.

Handcrafting with flowers can produce so many different and varied results. With *Floral Crafts for the first time* as a guide, your floral designs can complement any decorating scheme or convey any sentiment. Depending on the type of flowers (fresh, dried, or silk), the arrangement can last a week or be enjoyed all year long.

Creating the finished projects shown in this book may take some time and practice, since this is your first time working with flowers. However, once the twelve basic techniques of floral crafting are mastered, the possibilities of creating beautiful floral designs are endless.

How to use this book

For the person who is arranging flowers for the first time, this book provides a comprehensive guide to supplies, tools, and techniques that can be used to create not only fabulous decorative designs but also functional or necessary floral pieces.

Section 1: Floral Craft Basics familiarizes you with the basic tools and supplies you need to begin.

Section 2: Techniques contains instructions for twelve projects that can be made using basic floral-crafting techniques. Each technique builds on that which was learned in the previous technique from designing a basic arrangement in a vase to crafting with dried and silk florals.

Section 3: Projects Beyond the Basics expands on the techniques learned in Section 2 with eighteen additional projects that are a bit more complex and some-times combine two or more techniques.

Section 4: Art of Flowers features a variety of ways to display flowers and offers a glimpse at untraditional materials like beaded and metal flowers.

The purpose of *Floral Crafting for the first time* is to provide a starting point and to teach basic skills. The more you practice, the more comfortable you will feel. Allow yourself a reasonable amount of time to complete your first project—remember this is your first time. You will soon dis-cover that the techniques are easy to master.

After you have completed the first few projects, you will be surprised by how quickly you will be able to finish the re-maining projects. Take pride in the talents you are developing and the unique de-signs only you can create.

Section 1: *floral craft basics*

What do I need to know about fresh floral materials?

Paring Knife

Pocket Knife

Kitchen Knife

Stem Stripper

Floral Pruning Shears

Floral Shears

Wire Cutters

Heavy-duty Pruning Shears

To begin crafting with fresh florals, simply take a trip to the local craft store or florist to find a wide array of supplies. You may already have many of the supplies around the house.

Cutting Tools

The most essential tool in fresh florals is a sharp cutting tool. A cutting tool is vital for cleanly cutting the ends of a variety of stems before arranging them. The cutting tools used to create the projects in this book include:

Floral Pruning Shears—used for cutting thick fibrous stems, and for thin woody stalks such as azaleas, hydrangeas, etc. The blades must be sharp in order to make a clean cut.

Floral Shears—used for cutting most flower stems. The blades should be thin and very sharp to make a clean cut. Avoid using standard scissors to cut flowers. Standard scissors have thicker blades and will close the stem partway when cutting, impairing water absorption.

Hammer (not shown)—used for splitting thick woody stalks, and branches for better water absorption.

Heavy-duty Pruning Shears—used to cut and split thick stalks and branches.

Kitchen Knife—used to cut floral foam.

Paring Knife—used to trim thorns, leaves, and small stalks from the main stem.

Pocket Knife—used to trim thorns and leaves from the main stem.

Stem Stripper—used to clean thorns, leaves, and small stalks from the main stem.

Wire Cutters—used to cut floral wire.

Supports

The type of support you use will be dictated by the style of arrangement you will design. Certain supports such as floral foam and pin frogs may block some water absorption by the flower's stem and therefore should only be used when a certain style of floral arrangement is desired, or called for by the instructions. Floral supports used to create the designs in this book include:

Floral Clay Adhesive (not shown)—used to hold floral support in place.

Floral Foam—is dense green foam that is saturated and used to hold each stem in place. Soak foam in water before placing in container and inserting flower stems. After arrangement is complete and during the life of the arrangement, make certain to keep the foam damp.

Floral Foam in Plastic Grid—supports flowers, props, and foliage that can dry naturally in the arrangement.

Floral Foam

Wire Mesh

Floral Foam in Plastic Grid

Miscellaneous Supports

Pin Frog

Miscellaneous Supports—hold stems in place and make a pretty addition to a transparent glass vase. These supports include marbles, pebbles, plastic fillers, rocks, seashells, tumbled glass, etc.

Pin Frog—holds each stem in place.

Stalks—hold stems in place in any container.

Stems with Thorns (not shown)—create a natural support for a flower arrangement. The thorns will hold stems together, so other flowers added will also be held in place.

Wire Mesh—holds flowers in a general area without blocking their water supply. Chicken wire is most effective when secured around the top of the container.

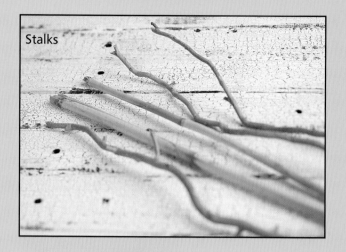

Stalks

Stalk Tip: A stem can be wedged or propped against a stalk for support.

Wire Mesh Tip: Wire mesh wedged into the container as shown at right adds a metallic element to the water to which the flowers may react. It can also damage stems, further contaminating the water.

14

Thread and Twine—help keep flowers in place and looking tidy. They can also be used to tie a grouping of flowers together in an arrangement.

Floral Tape—helps to give a stem additional support. It also helps in hiding supplemental floral wire and aids in preventing air pockets. Floral tape is soft enough to tear; however, waterproof floral tape requires the aid of craft scissors.

Floral Wire—is used to secure flowers or aid in bending a flower a certain way to make it fit better into an arrangement. Floral wire can also add length to stems of silk or dried flowers that are too short for an arrangement. Floral wire comes in gauges from 16 to 30. Floral wire will either be on a paddle or straight 18" lengths. The lower the gauge number, the thicker the wire will be. Make certain to use a gauge that will hold the flower, but not break the stem.

How do I care for fresh flowers?

Care and Conditioning of Flowers

Care and conditioning of fresh flowers are an essential part of floral crafting. Many factors such as container, light, temperature, water, and type of flowers play a part in how long a flower or its arrangement lasts. When working with fresh flowers, use the following method:

1. Make certain the container for the flowers and the water are clean. Once the flowers are placed into water, they begin to decompose or break down by releasing gases and forming bacteria. The cleaner the water, the less decomposition occurs, and the longer the flowers will last.

2. Clean flower stems before placing them in water. Remove leaves and stems that will be below the water level.

3. Place stems in the deepest water possible to promote container life. Water can be absorbed from the outside part of stem as well as the base. A nick or crack in the stem left exposed above water level can create an air pocket and block water flow to the flower. The deeper the water, the less likely this is to occur.

Care and Conditioning Tips:

• Place poisonous flowers such as daffodil or foxglove alone in their own container. These flowers secrete latex that is harmful to other flowers. They can be conditioned by standing them in deep water with a drop of bleach for 24 hours before mixing with other flowers.

• Mist flowers with cold water a few times a day to cool them. Flowers can also absorb the extra moisture through their petals.

• Keep flowers out of direct light.

• Keep flowers in a place with good airflow.

• Keep flowers away from smoke of any kind. Smoke is very harmful to flowers.

• Place flowers next to a window or in a cool room at night. It is not recommend to place flowers in the refrigerator at night. Many foods cause a negative reaction in the flowers from the gases that they release.

• Leave purchased cut flowers wrapped in paper or cellophane and place in deep water for an hour before arranging. This will ensure the flowers will be upright. Using sharp floral shears, trim at least 1" from bottom of stems.

- Pinch or trim off spent blossoms and leaves, encouraging other blossoms to open and helping the flowers last longer. The spent blossoms take some of the flower's energy to stay alive. Trimming these away allows the flowers to channel the energy to the healthy parts.

- Cut tips from flower stalks with graduating blossoms, such as gladiolas and snapdragons, to encourage other blossoms to open more quickly. This does not alter the natural appearance of the flower, but is helpful in speeding the blooming process.

- Avoid placing flowers directly into containers that are metal, rusted, or made of clay or stone. These materials are porous, and may contain elements that are harmful to flowers. It is best to line your container with an inner container of glass or plastic.

- Clean and sterilize containers to ensure extended vase life of the flowers.

Light

Flowers last longer in a place of low indirect light. Light creates heat and speeds up the life cycle of the flower. However, flowers with a green tinge owing to early cutting, or tightly budded flowers and branches, will need a strong light source to develop. Once the flowers show full color, put them in a place with less light. Many flowers will open in the light. This does not mean they are not fresh. It is the nature of certain flowers, which will close again in the dark.

Temperature

Warmer temperatures will cause flowers to open, and cooler temperatures will cause them to close. Flowers last longer if stored before arranging in temperatures around 45°F. Do not place arrangements by heat or air conditioner vent.

Water

Pure, clean water is best for flowers. Some elements in tap water can be harmful for flowers, such as too much fluoride or iron. A water purifier attached to the faucet will help.

Other methods of prolonging flower life, such as adding sugar, soda water, aspirin, or pennies to a vase are not recommended. The best method is a commercial floral additive available at the florist or craft store.

Tools such as a meat baster or narrow-spouted watering can are used to keep containers filled and stems in deep water. These tools make it easy to fill containers that have several stems or branches.

Misters are also recommended to cool flowers temporarily while providing an extra source of moisture.

17

Types of Flowers

All same-type flowers in a vase or container will last longer than a mixture of different types. Same-type flowers will decompose by the same means at the same pace. A single flower in a vase or container will last longer than several of the same type.

Different flowers have different composites and decompose by different means. This mixed reaction can shorten the life of all the flowers. When mixing flowers, change the water often.

Containers

Glass and plastic are the best materials to contain flowers. An assortment of plastic or glass containers in various sizes is necessary for proper hydration of floral arrangements. Containers should be clean and sterile before using them.

For decorative purposes, almost any container will work for flowers, from an antique paint can to an elegant crystal vase. The choice of container will influence the appearance of the arrangement. Containers should be as deep as possible, considering the length of the flower stem.

Reviving Fresh Flowers

Flowers may bend or droop due to light, temperature changes, or simply because it is the nature of the flower. Some flowers bend or droop because their heads become too heavy for their stems. The stems become waterlogged and stop conveying water to the flower head. Flowers can be revived using the following methods:

Method 1

1. Place flowers one by one before styling the arrangement on dampened newspaper or coated paper, lining them up evenly.

2. Gently roll dampened paper around flowers, forming a cone shape.

3. Secure paper with twine or with staples so that the paper braces the flowers.

4. Mist flowers and paper to keep them damp. Place cone of flowers in deep water for several hours.

5. Unwrap and arrange revived flowers.

Method 2

1. Cut stems shorter or place them into slightly warmer water. This helps the flower absorb water more quickly.

Method 3

1. Mist flowers while in arrangement with cold water several times each day. Remove arrangement to an area where water will not damage surface.

Method 4

1. Using a straight pin, prick flower just below the head, releasing air and increasing the water flow.

Troubleshooting for Fresh Flowers

When learning a new craft, mistakes and problems will occur. However, certain problems tend to be more common than others. Most problems can be corrected through knowing what went wrong. Following are troubleshooting methods for fresh floral crafts:

Water appears cloudy or discolored

Filmy water indicates decomposition of stem and bacterial growth in water. Change the water in container at least every couple of days. Use fresh warm water to open the stems, allowing water to flow to the flower.

Stems are discolored and filmy

This indicates that stems have been stagnating in water, impairing water absorption. Recut stems each time water is changed, allowing water to flow to the flower.

What do I need to know about dried floral materials?

Fire-retardant Spray

Floral Craft Foam

Container

Floral Shears

Dried Florals

Wire Cutters

Floral Tape

Glue Gun/Glue Sticks

Floral Wire

Dried flowers were once used chiefly as a winter substitute for fresh flowers. However, today's technology of preserving plant materials has resulted in the perpetual use of a wide variety of dried flowers.

Dried floral materials are natural materials that have been dehydrated so that they will last for long periods of time. These materials can be purchased at your local craft store or you can dry the floral materials personally.

To begin crafting with dried florals, simply take a trip to the local craft store or florist to find a wide array of supplies. You may have many of the supplies around the house.

Dried Floral Materials

Container—used to hold florals while drying as well as to display dried crafts. Refer to Containers on page 18.

Dried Florals—come in many various forms such as flowers, leaves, and vines. They are offered at your local craft store, garden center, and florist shop.

Fire-retardant Spray—used on dried materials that will be near candles or fireplaces.

Floral Craft Foam—used to secure dried materials in place. It is available in grayish-brown blocks. Floral craft foam is softer than floral Styrofoam® to prevent the delicate dried stems from breaking.

Floral craft foam can be secured to containers in several ways, depending on the container. The simplest method is to wedge the foam firmly into the container. Another method is to adhere it into the container.

The height of the floral craft foam in a dried arrangement depends on whether the arrangement is vertical or horizontal. If making a vertical arrangement, the foam should be ½" to ¾" below the rim of the container. If making a horizontal arrangement, the foam should be even or extend slightly above the rim of the container.

Floral Pins (not shown)—used to secure dried moss in place.

Floral Sealer (not shown)—used to enhance the color of dried materials and help hold delicate petals in place. Also, used as a sealer to help prevent the absorption of moisture.

Floral Shears—used for cutting dried materials.

Floral Tape—used to secure floral foam.

Floral Wire—used to secure dried materials together. Floral wire can also add length to stems that are too short for an arrangement.

Glue Gun/Glue Sticks—used to adhere dried materials onto arrangement. Low-temperature glue guns and glue sticks specifically formulated for floral craft foam are recommended for dried floral materials.

Newspaper (not shown)—used to cover and protect work surface.

Wire Cutters—used to cut floral wire.

Drying Flowers

Drying your own floral materials gives you a wider range of materials to work with when making floral arrangements. Floral materials can be air-dried or dried in silica gel.

Air-dried Flowers

Air-dried flowers can be dried with their stems attached. Air-dried flowers will be smaller than their original size. Also, the petals and leaves will have a withered appearance.

Most floral materials air-dry within five days to two weeks. There are several different methods of air-drying flowers. No matter which method you use, make certain that the location is dark, dry, and well ventilated. Test several locations around the house to find one that works best.

Method 1

1. Select flowers just before they reach full bloom. Remove lower leaves from stems.

2. Bundle flowers together loosely, staggering flower heads.

3. Secure bundle near ends of stems with rubber band, thread, or twine. Hang bundles upside down in a dark, dry, well-ventilated room where it will not be disturbed.

Method 2

1. Place 2" of water in container.

2. Remove lower leaves of floral materials. Place flowers upright into container. Allow water to evaporate naturally. *Note: The water slows their drying time and helps retain their original appearance.*

Method 3

1. Place wire mesh over deep box for flowers with long stems or shallow box for flowers with short stems.

2. Insert stems through mesh, allowing flowers heads to rest on wire mesh. *Note: This method works best for floral materials with large heads.*

23

Silica-Gel-Dried Flowers

Silica-gel-dried flowers are dried without stems. This method of drying helps the flowers retain the appearance of fresh flowers and remain close to their original shape and size. Silica gel can be reused several times.

Method 1

1. Cover work surface with newspaper.

2. Select flowers just before they reach full bloom. If using flowers from your garden, select and pick them when they contain the least amount of moisture. Garden flowers contain the least amount of moisture in the late morning or late afternoon.

3. Cut stem to within 1" of heads.

4. Remove lid from container. Fill container with 1½"–2" depth of silica gel.

5. Place flowers face up in silica gel. Gently sprinkle silica gel between flower petals. Cover flowers completely with silica gel. Cover tightly with lid. Allow to dry for 2–7 days.

6. Remove flowers from silica gel by tipping container and gently pouring out some of the silica gel onto a newspaper. Using slotted spoon, gently lift flowers from silica gel.

7. Using a soft brush, remove excess silica gel from flower and flower petals.

8. Spray flowers with floral sealer.

9. Dry and store silica gel, following manufacturer's instructions.

How do I care for dried florals?

Time, sunlight, moisture, and dust will take their toll on dried floral materials. The average shelf life of a dried floral arrangement is approximately one year. However, there are a few safeguards to preserve and extend its shelf life.

• Spray dried floral materials with a floral sealer before creating a floral craft, since they are so fragile.

• Avoid placing dried floral crafts in direct sunlight.

• Avoid placing dried floral crafts in bathrooms and window ledges because of condensation.

• Dust dried floral crafts with a hair dryer on a low setting.

Dried Floral Craft Tips:

• Cover work surface with newspaper.

• Work near an electrical outlet so that your glue gun will be within reach.

• Store dried materials by hanging them in bunches. A dowel or hook makes for a decorative as well as useful hanger.

• Store dried flower heads in a cardboard box cushioned with tissue paper. Place a small amount of silica gel into bottom of box to absorb any moisture.

• Separate bunches of dried materials by holding them over steam for 1–2 minutes. Remove from steam and gently pull apart.

What do I need to know about silk floral materials?

Silk is the general term used to describe any artificial floral material including silk, polyester, parchment, or latex. What silk floral materials lack in fragrance, they make-up for in adaptability and longevity. Most silk florals have wire stems, making them easy to work with when creating a floral craft.

To begin crafting with silk florals, simply take a trip to the local craft store to find a wide array of supplies. You may already have many of the supplies around the house.

Silk Floral Materials

Container—used to hold and display silk crafts. Refer to Containers on page 18.

Craft Glue—used to adhere stems into floral Styrofoam.

Floral Pins—used to secure ribbon and moss on silk floral crafts.

Floral Styrofoam®—used to secure silk materials in place. It can be secured to containers in several ways, depending on the container. The simplest method is to wedge the floral Styrofoam firmly into the container. Another method is to adhere the floral Stryrofoam into the container.

Floral Tape—used to cover silk floral stems and floral wire that is used to add length to silk floral stems.

Floral Wire—used to stabilize and lengthen silk floral stems that are too short for an arrangement.

Glue Gun/Glue Sticks—used to adhere silk materials onto arrangement. Low-temperature glue guns and glue sticks specifically formulated for floral Styrofoam are recommended for silk floral materials.

Newspaper (not shown)—to cover and protect work surface.

Pin Frog—aids in holding heavy silk flowers in place.

Ozone-safe Silk Floral Cleaner (not shown)—used to clean and freshen the color on silk materials.

Silk Florals—come in many various forms such as flowers, leaves, and vines. They are offered at your local craft store.

Sheet Moss—used to conceal the floral foam.

Wire Cutters—used to cut silk floral materials and floral wire.

How do I care for silk florals?

Silk florals require little maintenance, which is what makes them so appealing. However, there are a few safeguards in preserving their appearance.

• Avoid placing silk floral crafts in direct sunlight, because they will eventually fade.

• Dust silk floral crafts with a soft clean rag or with a hair dryer on a low setting. Silk floral materials can also be washed with warm soapy water. However, this is not recommend if mixed with dried florals or if the arrangement is in floral Styrofoam. An ozone-safe silk floral cleaner can be purchased in your local craft store. This will dissolve the dust and freshen the color. Make certain to read the manufacturer's label. Some sprays can damage plastic ornamental elements that may be mixed with silk floral materials.

Silk Floral Craft Tips:
• Work near an electrical outlet so that your glue gun will be within reach.

• Dip stems of silk florals into craft glue before inserting them in floral Styrofoam. This helps to secure them.

• Try to turn wire spines of leaves away from the viewer.

• Position or curve silk floral materials as they would naturally grow.

• Use varying stages of flower development to create a more natural look. For example, use rose buds as well as fully bloomed roses.

• Store silk floral materials upright in a cardboard box to prevent materials from being flattened or wrinkled. Place floral Styrofoam in cardboard box, then insert flower stems into floral Styrofoam. Secure box lid.

How do I design my floral arrangement according to where it will be displayed?

Fresh flowers from the garden placed randomly in a vase, a grand and very formal silk arrangement, or an antique serving tray with pressed pansies—all are part of the art of working with flowers. Unlike the traditions and styles of years past, whatever we want to do with flowers and the arranging of them are no longer restricted by rigid rules, subject to stringent guidelines, or dictated by fashion and style. Working with flowers has become a personal expression of sentiment, beauty, or design. However, there are a few design tips that are used by the "professionals" that may make your arrangements easier to accomplish and mirror the vision you had in your mind.

Proportion and Scale

• When making a floral arrangement or craft, consider where it will be placed. For a floral piece to have the proper proportion, the size (width and height) and quantity of the flowers should relate to the space it needs to fill and to the size of the container selected for that space. For example, a floral arrangement for a formal dining table should not interfere with the dinner served to guests. If the arrangement is too tall, the guests cannot speak to those across the table or if the piece is too large there will not be adequate room on the table for the serving dishes.

• Decide in the beginning if the arrangement will be seen from all sides or placed against a wall. It matters in the number of flowers that will need to be purchased to complete the arrangement.

• Determine the height then width of the arrangement. As a general rule, the height of the floral arrangement should be one-and-a-half to two times the height of the container

used. The width of the floral arrangement is usually, but not necessarily, approximately the same as the height.

• Visualize what the finished floral arrangement will look like before beginning.

Type of Arrangement or Craft
Formal Arrangement
Formal floral arrangements are usually larger and contain a substantial number of diverse, more elegant flowers that are "arranged" in some type of design style. Traditionally, a formal style is an arrangement that peaks in the center and is wider

and symmetrical on both sides. The flowers on each side are arranged identically and appear to be deliberately placed.

Informal Arrangement
An informal arrangement is one that looks as if its design element might have "just happened" during the arranging of the flowers. There is no specific sequence to the flowers, the flowers are more natural, and the container can be almost anything.

Correct Containers
Containers are often as important to the floral arrangement as the flowers themselves. Traditionally, containers were glass or porcelain vases that were made specifically for floral arrangements. Today, however, anything that will hold flowers is considered a container. It could be a wine glass, a milk bottle, or a rusty old urn. The only container criteria today is that you like it and it "fits" where you want it to go.

Balance
Balance is achieved when flowers are correctly positioned and secured in the container. This makes the final piece visually attractive and prevents it from falling over.

Symmetrical balance is achieved by positioning the flowers in the container so that the arrangement can be divided down the center, creating two halves that look alike.

Asymmetrical balance is achieved by positioning flowers in the container so that when the arrangement is divided down the center the two halves look different with equal visual weight on both halves.

Flower Size
Large flowers have more visual weight than small flowers. However, several small flowers grouped together can achieve the visual weight of one large flower.

Flower Color
The colors of the flowers placed in an arrangement have an aesthetic effect on the finished arrangement. Choose colors that complement or contrast with the colors of the room. Make certain that the flower colors are slightly lighter or slightly darker than the room. Light-colored flowers have less visual weight than dark-colored flowers. It may take two light-colored flowers to give the same visual weight of one dark-colored flower.

Type of Flower
One type of flower can be easily substituted for another if the flowers have the same line, size, or texture.

Floral Arranging Tips:

• Begin the floral arrangement by building the framework of the design with flowers or foliage.

• Build the floral arrangement from the inside, working outward. And then go back to the inside to fill in any holes that may have occurred.

• Choose a flower or leaf as your focal point and build around it.

• Cut some flower stems shorter to create depth.

• Add flowers and foliage for balance then fill in arrangement with remaining flowers and foliage.

• Distribute flowers of one type throughout the arrangement, unless it is a small flower that can be grouped together.

• Step back and look at the arrangement from various angles. Make adjustments as necessary.

Section 2: *techniques*

How do I cut fresh flower stems?

To keep your fresh flowers as beautiful as possible for as long as possible, it is essential to know how to cut fresh flower stems. Something as basic as how to cut different types of flower stems makes a big difference in the vase life of the arrangement.

What You Need to Get Started:

Florals
   Daisies: yellow
   Feverfew: white
   Peonies: white
   Snapdragons: white
   Sweet peas
   Waxflowers: pink

Supplies
   Clear vase
   Floral shears
   Water

Natural Bouquet

Here's How:

1. Refer to How do I design my floral arrangement according to where it will be displayed? on pages 28–29.

2. Fill vase ⅓ full with water.

3. Measure and cut stems of flowers, using the following techniques and the appropriate Cutting Tools from pages 12–13:

a. Trim off all leaves and thorns that will be below water level in vase. Allowing such materials to decompose in water will cause harmful bacteria and shorten the vase life of the flowers.

b. Hold flower near vase and at edge of work surface, with stem hanging below work surface to measure stem length against vase.

Continued on page 34.

3a.

3b.

Continued from page 32.

c. Always cut stems at a sharp angle. This increases surface area of stem and allows water to be better absorbed. Stems cut at an angle will not rest flush against the bottom of the vase.

3c.

Thick stems

d. Thick stems, stalks, and thin branches should be cut at an angle, then cut ½" up the center for better water absorption through the fibrous stems.

e. Hammer thick woody stalks and branches about 5"–6" up from bottom, making several splits in the stems. This allows for better water absorption.

3e.

f. Remove excess bark from split part of stalk to prevent water contamination. This will prolong the vase life of the flowers.

g. Immediately after end of each stalk or stem is cut, place it directly into water. It only takes a minute for the stalk to dry and seal up.

Hollow stems
Note: Hollow stems will crack and break more easily than solid stems.

h. Support hollow stems by slowly inserting a clean branch or stalk into end of stem.

Stems of branching or spray flowers
Note: Branching or spray flowers will last longer if separated.

i. Separate stems at their base, allowing water to be directly absorbed by each blossom. *Note: Spray flowers have very short stems when cut from their base, making arrangements possible only in a very small vase.*

3i.

Stems that secrete sap or latex

Note: Some flowers secrete sap or latex when cut. Singeing the ends will keep this fluid contained in the stem. The fluid is what the flower needs to last.

j. Using a candle with an extra-thick wick, singe about one-half of base of stem.

3j.

Fresh Floral Variation: A simple arrangement of tulips, with stems left long and leaves intact, is quite becoming in a white ceramic vase.

Stems with separations or nodes

Note: Some flowers such as carnations and dahlias have separations or nodes along their stems. The stem is thicker and more fibrous at these parts.

k. Cut stem between nodes to allow water to penetrate stem.

4. Arrange flowers, using the following method:

a. Position snapdragons in vase first.

b. Position feverfew, Waxflowers, and peonies around rim at base of snapdragons.

c. Position tall daisies and sweet peas to add height and depth to arrangement.

d. Position short-stemmed flowers last to avoid damage from arranging.

5. Fill vase with water until full.

Fresh Floral Variation: Using same-type flowers creates an entirely different design style even when simply arranged.

How do I wire fresh flowers for head support in an arrangement?

What You Need to Get Started:

Florals
Chrysanthemums
Gerbera daisies:
    orange;
    yellow
Hydrangea: pink
Peonies: pink
Roses: orange;
    yellow

Supplies
Ceramic vase
Floral shears
Floral tape
Floral wire:
    21-gauge
Water
Wire cutters

Giving the flower stems in an arrangement the necessary support to stand upright, or bend in a desired pose, can be done with the assistance of floral wire. Effectively wiring fresh flowers takes a little practice, but the methods are not difficult to master.

All Wired Up

All Wired Up

Here's How:

1. Refer to How do I design my floral arrangement according to where it will be displayed? on pages 28–29.

2. Fill vase ⅓ full with water.

3. Measure and cut stems of hydrangea to desired lengths. Refer to Technique 1, Step 3a–c on pages 32–34. Position in vase.

4. Measure and cut stems of peonies to desired lengths. Position in vase.

5. Wire remaining floral stems, using the following techniques:

Wiring for firm stems

Note: Occasionally the weight of a flower head necessitates the wiring of a stem to prevent premature drooping.

a. Using wire cutters, cut wire to length of stem.

b. Insert wire approximately ¼" into calyx and head, avoiding the seed pod.

5b.

c. Wind wire down along stem. At 1" from bottom of stem, bend wire back up toward the bloom and close it around stem.

d. Wrap stem and wire with floral tape.

5d.

e. Position in vase.

Wiring for delicate stems

f. If stem is too fragile, like a Gerbera daisy, wind floral wire around a similar sized dowel. Carefully remove from dowel, then slide wire onto stem.

g. Insert wire approximately ¼" into calyx and head.

5g.

h. Wrap stem and wire with floral tape.

i. Position in vase.

Wiring for additional stem length

j. Insert floral wire into stem and out through head of flower.

5j.

k. Bend floral wire into a hook and pull back into head. If wiring for stem length, make certain flower stem still has access to water.

5k.

l. Wrap stem and wire with floral tape.

m. Position flower in vase.

6. Fill vase with water until full.

Wiring Tip: Wiring for stem length can be used on artificial and dried flowers as necessary.

Fresh Floral Variation: The various flowers in this arrangement have been wired for head support.

Fresh Floral Variation: It is sometimes most effective to wire the accent flowers of a bouquet and leave the main part of the bouquet to fall naturally.

3
technique

**What You Need
to Get Started:**

Florals
Ivy
Roses: lt. pink
Statice: white
Sweet peas:
white
Viburnum: white

Supplies
Clear glass vase
Floral clay
adhesive
Floral shears
Floral tape
Floral wire:
24-gauge
Marbles
Paring knife
Pin frog: to fit in
vase
Water
Wire cutters

How do I make an arrangement using a pin frog for support?

A good, solid base is the best way to support a floral arrangement. Several different devices can be used as a base. A pin frog fits into the bottom of the vase or container and provides stability for long-stemmed flowers.

Perfect Pastels

Perfect Pastels

Here's How:

1. Refer to How do I design my floral arrangement according to where it will be displayed? on pages 28–29.

2. Prepare pin frog, using the following technique:

a. Apply floral clay adhesive to bottom of pin frog for added stability. Position in bottom of vase.

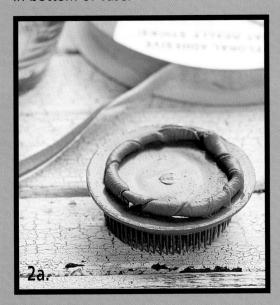

3. Fill vase ⅓ full with water.

4. Measure and cut stems of roses to desired lengths. Refer to Technique 1, Step 3a–c on pages 32–34.

5. Wire and wrap roses. Refer to Technique 2, Step 5a–d on page 37.

6. Position tallest roses in vase first, anchoring them in pin frog. Continue measuring, cutting, and positioning roses as desired.

7. Measure and cut stems of remaining flowers to desired lengths.

8. Position viburnum and statice in areas between roses, anchoring them on pin frog.

9. Position sweet peas to fill in arrangement, anchoring them in other stems.

10. Position ivy as an accent.

11. Add marbles to cover up pin frog.

12. Fill vase with water until full.

Silk Floral Variation: Pin frogs are also ideal for silk flowers. In the arrangement pictured here, the stems of these lovely silk flowers are secured on a pin frog.

Dried Floral Variation: Dried florals with heavy stems also can be placed on a pin frog. Care must be taken not to break stems.

4
technique

**What You Need
to Get Started:**

Florals
  Carnations: red
    variegated
  Hypericum

Supplies
  Craft scissors
  Floral foam
  Floral shears
  Floral tape
  Floral wire
  Kitchen knife
  Metal container:
    oblong
  Shallow pan
  Water
  Waterproof floral
    tape
  Wire cutters

How do I make an arrangement using floral foam?

Another material used to support a flower arrangement is floral foam. It is easily cut and made to fit into almost any container, or it can be used on a waterproof tray or dish. When moistened, floral foam keeps fresh flowers hydrated. Different types of floral foam are available for use with dried or silk floral crafts.

Country Carnations

Country Carnations

Here's How:

1. Refer to How do I design my floral arrangement according to where it will be displayed? on pages 28–29.

2. Prepare foam, using the following technique:

a. Using knife, cut foam to fit snugly into container. Place into container, making certain that it fits. Remove foam.

b. Immerse foam in shallow pan filled with water. Soak foam until saturated. Remove from water.

c. Position foam in container. Using craft scissors and waterproof floral tape, secure foam into container by placing strips of tape across top and securing on edges. *Note: The floral tape will be covered by the flowers.*

2c.

3. Measure and cut Hypericum stems to desired lengths. Refer to Technique 1, Step 3 on page 32.

4. Starting at center of the foam, position the Hypericum with the tallest stems first and cluster slightly shorter stems to the front and back.

5. Measure and cut stems of carnations to desired lengths.

6. Wire and wrap carnations. Refer to Technique 2, Step 5f–h on page 37.

7. Starting on top of floral foam, position a cluster of carnations with tallest stems and work shorter stems to the front and back. Continue, alternating Hypericum and carnations along length of container, clustering flowers at varied levels.

8. Place clusters of Hypericum and clusters of carnations along the sides, close to rim of container, at varied levels as desired.

9. Fill container with water until ¾ full. *Note: Stems will have forced some water out of the floral foam.*

Dried Floral Variation: This dried sunflower arrangement makes a great summer or fall decoration. Floral craft foam made for dried materials holds everything in place.

**What You Need
to Get Started:**

Florals
   Carnations:
      variegated
   Godetia: salmon
   Hypericum
   Irises: purple
   Larkspur: white
   Sprengeri fern
   Stargazer lilies:
      pink
   Viking pompons:
      yellow

Supplies
   Floral shears
   Floral tape
   Floral wire
   Wire cutters

How do I make a formal arrangement?

To create a formal arrangement, the technique of lacing is used. Lacing involves positioning the flowers in the vase, turning the vase 90°, and positioning more flowers. This helps to achieve a well-balanced symmetrical arrangement. Lacing allows stems to interlock and hold themselves in position.

Formally Yours

Formally Yours

Note: A formal arrangement is fairly symmetrical, so work from all sides of the vase.

Here's How:

1. Refer to How do I design my floral arrangement according to where it will be displayed? on pages 28–29.

2. Measure and cut stems of Sprengeri fern. Refer to Technique 1, Step 3a–c on pages 32–34.

3. Lace flowers, using the following technique:

a. Beginning with the shortest frond of Sprengeri fern, position stem in vase, allowing it to lean to one side. Repeat with second frond directly across from first.

b. Rotate vase 90° and position third stem between the first two stems. Position fourth stem directly across from third. *Note: Lacing allows stems to interlock and hold themselves in position.*

4. Measure and cut stems of larkspur and Stargazer lilies to desired length.

5. Lace larkspur and lilies in vase.

6. Measure and cut stems of Viking pompons to desired length. Lace in vase as desired.

7. Wire and wrap carnations. Refer to Technique 2, Step 5f–h on page 37. Lace in vase as desired.

8. Measure and cut stems of Hypericum to desired length. Position in vase as desired.

9. Measure and cut stems of Godetia to desired length.

10. Wire and wrap Godetia. Position in vase as desired.

11. Measure and cut irises to desired length. Position in vase as desired. *Note: Irises are positioned last because they are the most fragile of all the flowers used.*

Dried Floral Variation: This formal floral arrangement was created with dried florals, using a variation of the lacing technique. The stems are not interlocked in this arrangement because they have been inserted into floral craft foam. However, by rotating the container while positioning the flowers, the arrangement is kept symmetrical.

45

6 technique

Florals
Mini Pittosporum: variegated
Plastic berry spray: lt. yellow
Stocks: pink; white

Supplies
Bowl: large, shallow
Craft scissors
Finial: large
Floral shears
Hammer
Thread
Water
Wire cutters

How do I make an arrangement using foliage as a base?

Leafy foliage makes a handsome base for a floral arrangement. As seen in the photograph below, the green leaves offset the distinct shapes of the blossoms. The colorful pink and white stock seem to float atop the foliage, destined to be the focus of attention.

Blooms with Foliage

Blooms with Foliage

Here's How:

1. Refer to How do I design my floral arrangement according to where it will be displayed? on pages 28–29.

2. Place finial in bowl. If necessary, use a small bowl or glass to elevate finial to make certain that it will not be hidden by foliage.

3. Fill bowl ⅓ full with water.

4. Individually measure and cut mini Pittosporum stalks to desired lengths. Refer to Technique 1, Step 3a–g on pages 32–34.

5. Using craft scissors, cut 4" pieces of thread. Tie mini Pittosporum into groupings as needed. Position mini Pittosporum in bowl until a thick base has been formed.

6. Cut stock stems to length so that it rests above foliage.

7. Position stock in arrangement, making certain stem ends are in water.

8. Using wire cutters, cut berry sprays and position sparingly in arrangement.

9. Fill bowl with water until full.

Fresh Floral Variation: Carnations perched atop a cluster of graceful eucalyptus foliage make a casual yet stunning arrangement. Easy to assemble, the eucalyptus leaves act as an anchor for the delicate wired carnations.

47

technique

How do I make a dried arrangement using branches?

What You Need to Get Started:

Florals
Dried berry
  branches
Dried forsythia
  branches
Dried heather
  branches

Supplies
Craft knife
Heavy-duty
  pruning shears
Oriental-type
  vase: tall

Branches, both barren and blossom-covered, are a popular addition to floral arrangements. However, branches can also perform solo when given the opportunity. Since branches tend to stand rigidly upright, the vase will be in full view, making it a costar in the overall appeal of the arrangement.

Branching Out

Here's How:
1. Refer to How do I design my floral arrangement according to where it will be displayed? on pages 28–29.

2. Using craft knife, remove undesired or broken twigs, blooms, or foliage.

3. Measure branches to desired lengths. Using pruning shears, cut branches to desired lengths. *Note: If using live branches. Refer to Technique 1, Step 3a–g on pages 32–34.*

4. Position branches in vase. Continue measuring, cutting, and positioning branches as desired. *Note: If using freshly cut branches, make certain to place in water.*

Dried Floral Variation: Branches add interest and depth to any floral craft. These branches have been inserted into a wooden planter filled with pinecones and acrons.

8
technique

What You Need to Get Started:

Florals
Dried eucalyptus:
dk. green;
lt. green
Fresh pears
Plastic berry
sprays
Plastic fruit
sprays

Supplies
Floral foam
Floral picks
Floral shears
Floral wire:
21-gauge
Kitchen knife
Metal bucket:
tall, tapered
Wire cutters

How do I make an arrangement using ornamental elements and dried florals ?

Oftentimes a floral arrangement can be enhanced by adding ornamental elements not classified as foliage or flowers. These elements will need to be secured with floral wire or glue.

Pear Pleasure

Here's How:
1. Refer to How do I design my floral arrangement according to where it will be displayed? on pages 28–29.

2. Prepare floral foam so that it rests approximately 1" above bucket rim. Refer to Technique 4, Step 2a on page 43. *Note: Several pieces may need to be stacked for necessary height.*

3. Measure and cut eucalyptus stalks to desired lengths. Refer to Technique 1, Step 3a–g on pages 32–34.

4. Position eucalyptus in floral foam, working around bucket rim, allowing some eucalyptus to droop down.

5. Using wire cutters, cut desired elements from fruit spray and berry sprays. Position elements in arrangement. Secure with floral wire.

6. Insert a floral pick into the bottom of each pear. *Note: Floral picks come with wire attached to one end so that they can be secured to arrangement if pick is not long enough to reach the foam. Also, wire can be added for stem length. See Technique 2, Step 5j–l on page 38.*

6

7. Position pears in arrangement.

8. Position more eucalyptus, berries, and fruit to fill in arrangement.

9
technique

What You Need to Get Started:

Florals
Anthurium
Birds of Paradise (2)
Calycina
Isralia Ruscus
Leucadendron
Oncidium
Protea

Supplies
Bowl
Container: black, shallow
Floral foam
Floral shears
Water

How do I make an exotic fresh floral arrangement?

When working with any exotic flower, make certain to do your homework as they require special care. The flowers featured in this arrangement are Birds of Paradise. They do not continue to open after being cut. So, they must be opened manually. Even though exotic flowers require a little more maintenance, it is well worth your time.

Exotic Elegance

Here's How:
1. Refer to How do I design my floral arrangement or craft according to where it will be displayed? on pages 28–29.

2. Prepare floral foam. Refer to Technique 4, Step 2a–c on page 43.

3. Prepare Birds of Paradise.

a. Soak head of Bird of Paradise bloom in a bowl of lukewarm water for 5–7 minutes.

b. Working gently and starting at the back of the head, insert your thumb. Slide thumb forward and force blooms out of husk.

c. Remove white membranes and separate blooms until fully opened.

4. Measure and cut tallest Bird of Paradise stem to desired

3b.

3c.

length. Refer to Technique 1, Step 3a–c on pages 32–34.

5. Position and insert in center of floral foam until the stem reaches bottom of container.

6. Position and insert second Bird of Paradise slightly off center and in front of first Bird of Paradise.

7. Position Isralia Ruscus to form a visual line through center of floral design, providing horizontal length.

8. Position protea at base of Birds of Paradise.

9. Position and insert oncidium at front and back of Birds of Paradise, originating from center. *Note: This gives the illusion that all blooms are growing from one point.*

10. Layer Leucadendron in a step-like fashion at left of Birds of Paradise, descending toward floral foam. See photograph at right for placement.

11. Position and insert two Anthurium on the right side. Position and insert one Anthurium on the left, carrying the bright color across the design.

12. Fill in gaps with Calycina.

13. Fill container ¾ full with water. *Note: The larger stems will force much water out of the foam.*

Exotic Elegance

**What You Need
to Get Started:**

Florals
Carnations:
orange;
yellow

Supplies
Cotton crochet
thread
Craft scissors
Floral shears
Large-eyed sewing
needle

How do I string fresh flowers ?

Flowers are strung together using a large-eyed sewing needle and thread. By stringing fresh, silk, or dried flowers together, a beautiful lei or garland can be created. A lei as featured below can be worn, but it also can be used to as an accent for a room.

Lovely Lei

Lovely Lei

Here's How:

1. Refer to How do I design my floral arrangement according to where it will be displayed? on pages 28–29.

2. Using craft scissors, cut desired length of thread for lei, plus a few inches to allow for tying.

3. Insert single strand of thread through needle, then knot.

4. Using floral shears, cut off entire stem from carnation at the bottom of calyx.

5. Gently insert needle with thread up through center of calyx and bloom. Gently slide carnation down thread, working calyx into center of previous carnation.

6. Continue stringing and sliding onto thread, so as not to have space between blooms until desired look is achieved.

7. Remove needle and tie ends of thread together. Trim off excess.

Dried Floral Variation: The serenity of this monk statue is embellished with a strand of dried roses, loosely draped over his arms. Properly treated, this rosy garland will last in the elements of the outside garden. Dried, artificial, and fresh flowers can be strung and hung from mirrors, mantles, along tables, or almost anywhere.

Florals
Feverfew: white
Grapes: red
Lavender: white
Lemon leaves
Roses: cream

Supplies
Candle
Candleholder
Cardboard:
    24"-square
Floral preser-
    vative
Floral shears
Floral water
    vials/rubber
    tops
Paring knife
Silk evergreen
    wreath:
    18" dia.

How do I use a floral water vial?

Floral water vials are used to keep fresh flowers hydrated
when they cannot be placed in containers filled with water.
Water vials make it possible to use fresh flower accents in
places where keeping flowers fresh for more than a few hours
would be difficult.

Splendid Centerpiece

Splendid Centerpiece

Here's How:

1. Refer to How do I design my floral arrangement according to where it will be displayed? on pages 28–29.

2. Wash grapes and set aside to dry.

3. Place cardboard on flat work surface.

4. Prepare floral preservative mixture, following manufacturer's instructions. Fill each vial with preservative mixture and replace rubber top.

5. Measure and cut stems of roses to 6" in length. Immediately push stems into vials until immersed. Refer to Technique 1, Step 3c on page 34.

6. Trim ends of remaining florals to 6"–8" in length. Immediately push stems into vials until immersed.

7. Place wreath on cardboard square. Randomly insert feverfew, lavender, lemon leaves then roses into wreath, making certain that vials cannot be seen.

8. Trim remaining flowers as necessary. Insert flowers into wreath as desired.

9. Place grapes carefully around wreath with pointed ends of clusters draping over outside edge of wreath.

10. Carefully pick up cardboard square and centerpiece. Slide centerpiece off cardboard onto in desired location. Adjust centerpiece as necessary.

11. Place candleholder and candle in center of wreath. Light candle when guests arrive. *Note: Watch candles carefully, they may need to be replaced from time to time. Do not let candles burn down to less than 3" above flowers.*

Fresh Floral Variation: This tote filled with fresh items from the market and accented with daisies makes an extra-special gift. The daisies have been placed in water vials to prolong their vase life.

How do I make a silk floral arrangement in acrylic water?

What You Need to Get Started:

Florals
  Silk tulips: white

Supplies
  Acrylic water
  Clean disposable
    bowl
  Clean disposable
    spoon
  Clear expendable
    glass vase
  Paper towels

Acrylic water can create the illusion of a fresh arrangement in vase while using dried or silk materials. Simply, mix the acrylic water following manufacturer's instructions, and use your imagination.

Silk Style

Silk Style

Note: Acrylic water should be kept out of reach from children and animals.

Here's How:

1. Refer to How do I design my floral arrangement according to where it will be displayed? on pages 28–29.

2. Determine how much acrylic water is desired in vase. *Note: Acrylic water products can be purchased at your local craft store.*

3. In well-ventilated area and using a spoon, mix acrylic water in a bowl, following manufacturer's instructions.

4. Pour mixture into vase. Wipe up any spills immediately with a paper towel.

5. Arrange silk tulips in vase as desired. Continual adjusting of arrangement is required until acrylic water sets up.

6. Avoid disturbing vase for twenty-four hours.

Acrylic Water Tip: Make certain to use a vase or container that can be disposed of once arrangement is no longer wanted. Acrylic water cannot be removed from vase or container once it has set up.

Dried Floral Variation: When placing dried florals in acrylic water, make certain to handle with care. Otherwise, small dried pieces may break off and land in the acrylic water.

59

Section 3: *projects beyond the basics*

1
project

What You Need to Get Started:

Florals
Carnations:
  orange
Roses: yellow
  with orange
  edges
Sunflowers

Supplies
Floral shears
Floral tape
Floral wire:
  21-gauge
Glass container:
  tall, slender
Water
Wire cutters

How do I make an arrangement using a tall slender container?

The shapes and sizes of floral arrangement containers are limitless. A tried-and-true favorite is the tall, oblong container. Many overall effects are possible when using a tall, slender container for a floral arrangement. If the container is glass or shiny black porcelain, a more contemporary feel is obtained. For a more rustic approach, use a wooden or metal container.

Fall Fresh

Here's How:
1. Refer to How do I design my floral arrangement according to where it will be displayed? on pages 28–29.

2. Fill container ⅓ full with water.

3. Measure and cut all flower stems to desired lengths. Refer to Technique 1, Step 3a–c on pages 32–34.

4. Position sunflowers in vase first. *Note: Sunflowers have not been wired, adding a natural look to the arrangement.*

5. Wire and wrap carnations and roses. Refer to Technique 2, Step 5a–h on page 37.

6. Position carnations and roses in vase.

7. Fill container with water until full.

Silk Floral Variation: Simply enchanting, silk daisies playfully peek out of a glass container. The contrast between the dainty, airy blossoms and the tall, slender container becomes a delightful piece of country charm.

2
project

Florals
  Mini carnations:
    yellow
  Snapdragons:
    pink
  Sweetheart roses:
    dk. pink

Supplies
  Floral shears
  Floral tape
  Floral wire:
    21-gauge
  Glass beads
  Tiny glass
    vase
  Water
  Wire cutters

How do I arrange flowers in a small container?

Typically, flowers in smaller containers are arranged in very close proximity to each other, creating a dense bouquet effect. A technique called lacing is used to create the arrangement featured below. The flower stems are interlocked with each other, holding the flowers in position.

Itty-bitty Bouquet

Itty-bitty Bouquet

Here's How:

1. Refer to How do I design my floral arrangement according to where it will be displayed? on pages 28–29.

2. Fill vase ⅓ full with water. Fill vase ½ full with glass beads.

3. Measure and cut stems of mini carnations. Refer to Technique 1, Step 3a–c on pages 32–34.

4. Wire and wrap carnations. Refer to Technique 2, Step 5f–h on page 37.

5. Lace carnations around edge of vase. Refer to Technique 5, Step 3 on page 45.

6. Measure and cut stems of Sweetheart roses.

7. Wire and wrap Sweetheart roses. Refer to Technique 2, Step 5a–d on page 37.

8. Continue lacing stems of remaining carnations, alternating with Sweetheart roses as desired. Fill in gaps with snapdragon as desired.

9. Fill vase with water until full.

Fresh Floral Variation: A coffee mug makes an ideal container for a small fresh flower arrangement of roses and carnations. As shown above, such an arrangement looks and smells delicious enough to eat!

Ceramic Floral Variation:
As shown on the left, tiny ceramic roses are placed and tied together in bunches, then arranged in a small galvanized metal container. The result is a token of fanciful charm that will outlast the season.

How do I make an arrangement using a wire form?

What You Need to Get Started:

Florals
Carnations:
orange
Spanish moss

Supplies
Floral foam
Floral pins
Floral shears
Kitchen knife
Water
Wire pumpkin
form

Wire forms can be used to make a wonderfully imaginative flower arrangement. Find or make a wire form (such as the wire pumpkin used here) that suits the theme of the arrangement, add floral foam and moss, and the foundation for an extraordinary floral masterpiece has been created.

Flowering Pumpkin

Here's How:
1. Refer to How do I design my floral arrangement according to where it will be displayed? on pages 28–29.

2. Prepare floral foam. Refer to Technique 4, Step 2a–b on page 43.

3. Position floral foam in wire form.

4. Dip moss into water. Cover floral foam with dampened moss.

5. Using floral pins, secure moss to floral foam.

6. Measure and cut stems of carnations to desired lengths. Refer to Technique 1, Step 3a–c on pages 32–34.

7. Position carnations from the center, working out.

4
project

**What You Need
to Get Started:**

Florals
Pittosporum:
variegated

Supplies
Hammer
Heavy-duty
pruning shears
Rustic clay pot
Water

How do I make an arrangement using foliage without flowers?

A simple arrangement of foliage is often all that is needed to fill a bare spot. Remember not to limit yourself to only green foliage. Foliage comes in yellow, silver, and autumn colors.

Fabulous Foliage

Fabulous Foliage

Here's How:

1. Refer to How do I design my floral arrangement according to where it will be displayed? on pages 28–29.

2. Fill pot ⅓ full with water.

3. Measure and cut stalks of Pittosporum to desired length. Refer to Technique 1, Step 3a–g on pages 32–34.

4. Lace stalks. Refer to Technique 5, Step 3 on page 45.

5. Fill in gaps as desired.

6. Fill pot with water until full.

Dried Floral Variation: Dried lamb's ear is an excellent choice for making a foliage arrangement. Cascading down a rust vase, the leaves' complex shapes and textures are vivid.

Silk Floral Variation: Silk silver dollars have been inserted into glass vases. Foliage arrangements such as these can be used as centerpieces on a picnic table or added to a shelf next to your favorite pictures and books.

Florals
Carnations:
  red
Leucodendron
Mini carnations:
  red
Peppercorn:
  green
Potted live
  Anthurium:
  6" dia.
Snapdragons:
  pink

Supplies
Floral shears
Floral tape
Floral wire:
  21-gauge
Water
Wire cutters

How do I use fresh flowers with a potted plant to make an arrangement?

Make an arrangement more permanent by combining a potted plant with fresh flowers. The arrangement featured below offers an interesting selection of fresh flowers and a potted plant. The fresh flowers can be replaced as they begin to wilt.

Potted Posies

Potted Posies

Here's How:

1. Refer to How do I design my floral arrangement according to where it will be displayed? on pages 28–29.

2. Measure and cut all fresh flowers to desired lengths. Refer to Technique 1, Step 3a–c on pages 32–34.

3. Wire and wrap carnations. Refer to Technique 2, Step 5f–h on page 37.

4. Position carnations around base of potted Anthurium.

5. Position snapdragons, adding height and fullness.

6. Position Leucodendron and peppercorn in arrangement as desired.

7. Water potted Anthurium on a regular basis.

Silk Floral Variation: This silk ivy plant has had fresh white roses added to the top. Replace fresh flowers as they begin to wilt. Use fresh florals that match the color scheme of the room or an upcoming holiday season.

What You Need to Get Started:

Florals
Cushion pompons: yellow

Supplies
Angel food cake
Cake plate
Drinking glass to fit into center of cake
Floral shears
Frosting glaze: dk. yellow; lt. yellow
Water

How do I embellish food with florals?

Food can be embellished with florals in various ways such as placing a single flower next to an entrée, placing flowers on top of food, or inserting flowers into the food item. Fresh florals inserted into food will last only a few hours. However, the flowers on the cake featured below will last much longer because they are actually sitting in a glass of water.

Delightful Dessert

Delightful Dessert

Here's How:

1. Refer to How do I design my floral arrangement according to where it will be displayed? on pages 28–29.

2. Arrange cake on plate as desired.

3. Drizzle lt. yellow frosting over cake. Repeat with dk. yellow frosting.

4. Place glass into center of cake.

5. Fill glass ⅔ full with water.

6. Measure and cut stems of Cushion pompons to desired lengths. Refer to Technique 1, Step 3a–c on pages 32–34.

7. Position flowers in glass.

> **Edible Flower Tip:**
> Some flowers are edible and can be served with the cake. Make certain to research which flowers are edible and which are not. Edible flowers also can be sugared.

Fresh Floral Variation: This wedding cake was embellished with Italian Ruscus, ivy, and roses along with some icing flowers and icing leaves. Italian Ruscus in 4"–5" lengths cascade off the edge of the cake. Rose stems, cut to 1" lengths, were inserted immediately before displaying.

Fresh Floral Variation: While flowers make lovely wedding cake decorations in and of themselves, some very beautiful wedding cakes integrate porcelain statuettes, waterfalls, fill flowers (such as baby's breath), and greenery.

73

How do I make a fresh floral wreath?

Florals
   Ivy
   Leather fern
   Roses: pink
      purple
      yellow
   Tulips: white

Supplies
   Floral foam
      wreath: 8" dia.
   Floral shears
   Paring knife
   Shallow pan
   Water

A fresh floral wreath can be created using a floral foam wreath that has been saturated with water then inserting fresh florals. Two important guidelines in creating a fresh floral wreath are to assemble right before displaying and to mist wreath often. A wire hanger has been placed on the back of the fresh floral wreath on the facing page then carefully hung.

Fresh Floral Wreath

Note: Be aware that drainage of water may occur when fresh floral wreath is first hung.

Here's How:

1. Refer to How do I design my floral arrangement according to where it will be displayed? on pages 28–29.

2. Immerse wreath in shallow pan filled with water. Soak until it is saturated, then remove from water.

3. Measure and cut stems of roses and tulips to 2" in length. Refer to Technique 1, Step 3a and 3c on pages 32–34.

4. Evenly position roses and around front and sides of wreath and on each side of midline.

5. Evenly position tulips around front and sides of wreath as desired.

6. Measure and cut stems of Leather fern fronds and ivy to desired lengths. Evenly position fronds and ivy around roses and tulips in wreath.

How do I make a fresh floral arrangement using a candle?

**What You Need
to Get Started:**

Florals
  Hydrangea: blue
  Silk pansies

Supplies
  Candle: 3"-square
  Craft scissors
  Floral shears
  Floral wire:
    21-gauge
  Papier-mâché
    container: long,
    shallow
  Ribbon: 1"-wide
  Small jar with lid
  Water
  Wire cutters

A candle can be easily inserted into a floral arrangement. However, the floral arrangement featured below was actually designed around the candle. The candles in the dried floral arrangement on the opposite page were inserted at the last minute for an added touch. Remember to keep the flame of the candle away from any floral materials.

Glowing Floral

Glowing Floral

Here's How:

1. Refer to How do I design my floral arrangement according to where it will be displayed? on pages 28–29.

2. Fill container ⅓ full with water.

3. Center and place jar in container. Center and place candle on jar.

4. Measure and cut stems of hydrangea into small sprays. Refer to Technique 1, Step 3a, 3c, and 3i on pages 32–34.

5. Position small sprays around candle. Continue as desired.

6. Position silk pansies in arrangement.

7. Using craft scissors, cut desired length of ribbon for bow.

8. Make a bow and secure with wire.

9. Position bow at one end of arrangement away from candle.

10. Fill container with water until full.

3

Dried Floral Variation: The floral arrangement featured on the left contains dried pinecones, acorns, and leaves. Cream-colored candles and tanned leather pieces further accentuate the look of this rustic arrangement.

9
project

What You Need to Get Started:

Florals
- Dried mini allium sprays
- Dried myrtle sprays
- Plastic berry sprays: frosted
- Plastic plum sprays
- Silk cone hydrangeas: pink; purple
- Twig wreath: 36" dia.

Supplies
- Floral shears
- Glue gun/glue sticks
- Newspaper
- Wire cutters

How do I make a dried floral wreath?

A dried floral wreath makes a becoming year-round decoration either indoors or outdoors. An artistic mixture of dried floral materials, the wreath featured on the opposite page takes some time to assemble, but it will be well worth it.

Dried Fields

Here's How:

1. Refer to How do I design my floral arrangement according to where it will be displayed? on pages 28–29.

2. Cover flat work surface with newspaper.

3. Place wreath on work surface.

4. Position and glue hydrangeas around center of wreath, over-lapping to cover stems of previously glued flowers.

5. Cut myrtle into 10"–12" lengths. Position and glue myrtle around outside of hydrangeas.

6. Cut allium into small clusters of flowers. Position and glue clusters around wreath as desired.

7. Using wire cutters, cut plums into two- and three-plum clusters. Position and glue clusters around wreath as desired.

8. Position and glue berries around wreath as desired.

Large Wreath Tip: Make a hanger from wire to attach on back of wreath.

Dried Wreath Variation: The floral wreath shown above was created with dried florals such as twigs, sunflower heads, and wheat stock. A dried artichoke has been added for the finishing touch.

10
project

How do I make a spray using dried and silk materials?

What You Need to Get Started:

Florals
Dried honey-
  suckle vines
Dried mini lotus
  pods
Dried Nigella
  pods
Dried Papaver
  Giganthums
Dried pepper
  berries
Dried Plumosus
Dried Thika pods
Silk chrysanthe-
  mums:
  lt. peach (5)
Silk grape leaves

Supplies
Floral wire:
  18-gauge
Glue gun/glue
  sticks
Heavy-duty
  pruning shears
Newspaper
Wire cutters

Sprays can be made from fresh, dried, or silk floral material, or a combination thereof with the use of a glue gun and floral wire. Fastened together by a wire at the center, the honeysuckle vines form a gentle, graceful arch. The dried and silk floral materials are then glued into placed.

Spring Spray

Here's How:

1. Refer to How do I design my floral arrangement according to where it will be displayed? on pages 28–29.

2. Cover flat work surface with newspaper.

3. Using heavy-duty pruning shears, cut honeysuckle vines into arches of desired lengths.

4. Wire vines together at center. Using wire cutters, trim off excess wire.

5. Position and glue Plumosus in between vines until desired fullness is achieved for spray.

6. Position and glue grape leaves onto Plumosus.

7. Center and glue two chrysanthemums onto spray to create a focal point.

8. Position and glue remaining chrysanthemums onto spray as desired.

9. Position and glue pepper berries, Nigella pods, Papaver Giganthums, Lotus pods, and Thika pods onto spray as desired.

> **Spray Tip:** To make a long spray, create it in several sections. It is easier to produce the desired shape if each section is made separately, then wired together.

80

11

project

What You Need to Get Started:

Florals
Dried lavender flowers
Dried rosebuds
Nuts: assorted
Plastic berry sprays: yellow
Plastic fruit
Spanish moss

Supplies
Clay pot: 5¼" dia.
Craft glue
Craft scissors
Floral Styrofoam®
Glue gun/glue sticks
Kitchen knife
Newspaper
Satin ribbon: 1"-wide, variegated
Styrofoam® balls: 3"; 4"
Wooden dowel: ¼" dia., 11"

How do I make a dried floral topiary?

A dried floral topiary can be easily made with the use of floral Styrofoam, glue, and imagination. The topiary featured on the opposite page was made with Styrofoam balls that were rolled in dried lavender flowers. Various dried florals were then added to the topiary and the clay pot. Nestled on a shelf or centered on a table, a topiary like this is certain to capture the admiration of all who behold it.

Topiary Delight

Here's How:

1. Cover flat work surface with newspaper.

2. Prepare floral Styrofoam. Refer to Technique 4, Step 2a on page 43. Leave floral Styrofoam in clay pot.

3. Center and push dowel down into floral Styrofoam to bottom of pot.

4. Center and push 4" ball down onto dowel to top of pot. Center and push 3" ball down onto dowel to top of 4" ball.

5. Using glue gun, glue balls together and floral Styrofoam to pot.

6. Pull dowel up and remove. Spread craft glue on 4" ball. Sprinkle lavender flowers on glue. Press flowers into glue. Shake off excess flowers.

7. Repeat with 3" ball. Allow to dry.

8. Reinsert dowel through balls and floral Styrofoam.

9. Using glue gun, glue moss onto top of floral Styrofoam.

10. Position and glue dried rosebuds at base of each ball as desired.

11. Tie ribbon around pot and glue fruit, nuts, and berries onto pot as desired.

Topiary Tips: Turn the topiary regularly; this will ensure that it fades evenly. Be careful when turning the clay pots. They tend to have rough bases that may scratch or damage the surface.

The smaller topiaries featured on the shelf in the photograph at right have been created with dried rose buds and potpourri.

12

project

How do I make a fresh floral topiary?

A fresh floral topiary can be created using an ivy plant, wire basket, and monofilament. The ivy topiary featured on the opposite page has been embellished with light purple hydrangeas. The fresh flowers can be replaced as they wilt.

What You Need to Get Started:

Florals
Hydrangea: lt. purple
Potted live ivy with long trailers: 10" dia.
Sheet moss

Supplies
Craft scissors
Floral foam
Floral shears
Floral wire: 18-gauge
Monofilament
Paring knife
Shallow pan
Toothpicks
Water
Wire basket: 10" dia.
Wire cutters
Wooden dowels: ¼" dia., 24" (2)

Ivy Surprise

Here's How:
1. Refer to How do I design my floral arrangement according to where it will be displayed? on pages 28–29.

2. Carefully insert dowels 1" apart into center of potted ivy and down to bottom of pot.

3. Carefully bring 5–6 bases of the longest trailers up to base of dowels.

4. Using craft scissors, cut one 4" length from monofilament and tie around base of both dowels, securing bases of trailers between them.

5. Using floral shears and beginning at base of dowels, trim off ivy leaves along 14" section of each trailer.

6. Gently holding trailers between dowels, wrap moss around and up to top of dowels, creating a "pole" in center of plant.

7. Wrap entire pole with monofilament to hold moss in place. Tie off at top of pole.

8. Place wire basket on top of pole and secure with floral wire.

9. Wrap tops of trailers, with leaves attached, around framework of basket to fill it in.

10. Using paring knife, cut floral foam into an egg shape 3" in length. Immerse foam in shallow pan filled with water. Soak floral foam until saturated. Remove from water.

Continued on page 86.

Ivy Surprise

Continued from page 84.

11. Cut small sprays from hydrangea. Refer to Technique 1, Step 3c and 3i on page 34.

12. Using a toothpick, create small holes in floral foam egg where sprays will be placed. Position sprays in holes.

13. Continue cutting and positioning sprays into egg until completely covered.

14. Place egg in basket at top of topiary.

Silk & Dried Floral Variation: In the photograph at the left, dried heather sprays are gently wired to silk ivy that sits tall in an oval vase. A silk bow adds the finishing touch to this striking arrangement.

How do I make a wedding bouquet?

The two basic elements in creating most wedding bouquets are desired florals and ribbon. Wedding bouquets come in a wide variety of styles and sizes. The wedding bouquet featured below is a monochromatic cascade-style bouquet.

What You Need to Get Started:

Florals
Baby's breath
Leather fern
Mini carnations: white
Roses: white
Sprengeri fern

Supplies
Craft scissors
Floral foam bouquet holder with plastic handle
Floral shears
Floral tape
Floral wire: 18-gauge
Paring knife
Sheer satin ribbon: 1"-wide; white (1 yd)
Sink
Water
Wire cutters

Cascade-style Bouquet

Cascade-style Bouquet

Photograph on page 87.

Here's How:

Note: Consider the size and weight of arrangement before beginning. Someone may be holding this for hours.

1. Immerse holder in clean sink filled with water. Soak holder until floral foam is saturated. Remove from water.

2. Starting on top of holder, position Leather fern frond. Continue all around edges of holder. *Note: Make certain to position stems as deep as possible into floral form, ensuring that they will not work lose.*

3. Starting on bottom of holder, position a long-stemmed Sprengeri fern frond. Continue, adding progressively shorter fronds to the left and right. Position shorter fronds at sides and top, forming the perimeter of the bouquet.

4. Measure and cut stems of roses to desired lengths. Refer to Technique 1, Step 3a–c on pages 32–34.

5. Wire and wrap stems of roses. Refer to Technique 2, Step 3a–d on page 37.

6. Position longest rose stem in bottom of holder. Continue, adding progressively shorter pieces to the left and right, up the holder.

7. Measure and cut stems of mini carnations to desired lengths. Make certain to cut three long-stemmed mini carnations.

8. Wire and wrap stems of mini carnations. Refer to Technique 2, Step 3f–h on page 37.

9. Position mini carnations into center of holder and around edges, completing the shape. Position three long-stemmed carnations in bottom of holder, completing cascade.

10. Measure and cut stems of baby's breath to desired lengths.

11. Fill in gaps with baby's breath.

12. Using craft scissors, cut and tie ribbon into a bow, leaving long streamers. Insert floral wire through back loop of bow. Fold wire in half and twist halves together, creating a floral pick.

13. Position floral pick in bottom portion of bouquet, working the loops and streamers in between the flowers.

Wedding Bouquet Tip: Keep wedding bouquet cool and misted until ready to use.

Porcelain Floral Variation: These porcelain rosebuds have been gently wired onto an heirloom lace hankie for the bride to carry down the isle. A satin bow has been added for "something blue."

Fresh Floral Variation: The bouquet featured above is a perfect bouquet for a summer wedding. It has a wide variety of vividly-colored flowers such as Lisianthus, calla lilies, and mini Gerbera daisies.

Fresh Floral Variation: Wedding bouquets can be created using one type of flower. The bouquet in the photograph above features a blooming garden of roses.

Vintage Floral Variation: This unique wedding bouquet is a vintage metal candy box. It has been embellished with antique lace and vintage florals. A small plastic bouquet handle has been adhered to the bottom. Placed inside the candy box is something old, something new, something borrowed, and something blue.

How do I make a floral craft using miniature lights?

What You Need to Get Started:

Florals
Artificial
  Christmas
  tree
Plastic floral
  picks: assorted
Sheet moss
Silk roses

Supplies
Ceramic urn
Craft glue
Floral Styrofoam®
Floral wire:
  21-gauge
Miniature light
  set
Wire cutters

String miniature lights onto a floral craft arrangement, starting at the top so that the plug ends at the bottom back. Make certain that arrangement will be displayed by an electrical outlet. Miniature lights are not recommended for embellishment of fresh florals.

Floral Tree

Here's How:
1. Refer to How do I design my floral arrangement according to where it will be displayed? on pages 28–29.

2. Prepare floral Styrofoam. Refer to Technique 4, Step 2a. Leave floral Styrofoam in urn.

3. Position and insert trunk of tree into floral Styrofoam.

4. Glue sheet moss around tree trunk to cover floral Styrofoam.

5. Starting on top, string lights on tree as desired. *Note: It is best to have cord coming out of the back side of the tree.*

6. Position and wire roses onto tree. Trim off excess wire.

7. Position and wire plastic picks onto tree. Trim off excess wire.

Floral Tree Tip: Change the color of the roses and use different picks that help celebrate the upcoming season. Or decorate a tree to match the theme or color scheme of a room. It would also look great on a porch.

How do I make a naturally dried arrangement?

What You Need to Get Started:

Florals
Roses
Sheet moss

Supplies
Cellophane wrap
Clay pot: 5" dia.
Craft knife
Floral foam
Floral shears
Paring knife
Shallow pan
Water

Enjoy a fresh flower arrangement today and then the same arrangement later on, after it has dried. It is best to use the same type of flowers because they should dry at the same rate. Simply use damp foam for when the blooms are fresh, and after it dries out, the flowers begin their natural drying process. Dried flowers shrink a bit, so the dried arrangement will need some extra attention, such as adding supplemental dried flowers or greenery to fill in any gaps.

Dried Rose Essence

Here's How:
1. Refer to How do I design my floral arrangement according to where it will be displayed? on pages 28–29.

2. Prepare foam. Refer to Technique 4, Step 2a–b on page 43.

3. Line clay pot with cellophane wrap.

4. Position foam into pot.

5. Measure and cut roses to desired lengths. Refer to Technique 1, Step 3a–c on pages 32–34.

6. Position roses as desired into floral foam. Fill in as desired with sheet moss.

7. Place arrangement out of sunlight and humidity. Make certain air around arrangement is warm and dry.

8. Roses may shrink as they dry. Fill in with sheet moss, if necessary.

Dried Floral Variation: This dried arrangement was created with various colors of hydrangeas that were naturally dried in an urn.

16
project

What You Need to Get Started:

Florals
Dried baby's
  breath: pink
Dried mini roses:
  white
Sheet moss
Velvet leaves:
  green

Supplies
Craft scissors
Glue gun/glue
  sticks
Jewelry pin back
Lace: 1½"-wide
  (¾ yd)
Lightweight
  cardboard:
  2" x 3"
Sewing needle
Sewing thread:
  ivory (2 yds)
Small ivory seed
  beads: (1 hunk)

How do I make a jewelry pin using dried flowers?

With dried flowers, you can make jewelry pins of heirloom sentimentality in a small amount of time with dried florals, lace, and a glue gun. The floral pins featured on the opposite page combine dried materials with beads, and lace. Pins such as these, inspired by the Victorian era, add a touch of romance to a blouse, dress, or suit jacket.

Romantic Rose Pin

Here's How:
1. Wrap lace around cardboard, overlapping at back. Glue to secure.

2. Thread needle. Knot ends together. Insert needle and thread in lace at bottom of cardboard piece ½" from edge.

3. String enough beads onto needle and thread make a 1½" loop.

4. Secure thread in lace at bottom edge again, then string enough seed beads to make a 2¼" loop. Repeat until nine similar loops are formed, alternating 1½" loops with 2¼" loops. Knot thread to secure.

5. Glue sheet moss onto outer edges of lace front. Glue leaves over lace-covered cardboard, creating a base. See photograph at right.

6. Glue mini roses onto base. Fill in with dried baby's breath as desired.

7. Glue jewelry pin back horizontally onto back of lace-covered cardboard. Allow to dry.

Dried Floral Variation: The red rose pin featured at the top left is created by gathering threads on one edge of 1½"-wide cream lace and folding them under. The lace is pulled into a circle with the fullness distributed evenly. Edges are secured with glue. Slightly overlapped velvet leaves are glued to the center of circle along with statice and rose-buds. White beads are then glued onto arrangement and lace as desired. A jewelry pin glued onto cardboard has been glued onto back of lace circle.

What are some unique containers to display floral arrangements?

What You Need to Get Started:

Florals
Plastic pear with pick
Plastic pepper-berry sprays
Silk greenery: assorted
Silk roses
*Vintage cherry stems
Wooden-petal daisy

Supplies
Clay pots: 5" dia., green (3)
Craft knife
Floral Styrofoam® (3)
Floral wire: 21-gauge
Glue gun/glue sticks
Pliers
Wire cutters

*Vintage Floral Tip: Vintage florals can be found at your local antique stores. Plastic or silk florals can be substituted for vintage floral materials.

The various ways to display floral arrangements are endless from where you place the arrangement to what you display it in. The arrangement featured below was placed into three old clay pots that were painted and wired together. The container holding the arrangement on the opposite page was an old garden pot that was painted and embellished with seashells.

Tri-pot Bouquet

Tri-pot Bouquets

Here's How:

1. Refer to How do I design my floral arrangement according to where it will be displayed? on pages 28–29.

2. Place pots together with edges touching. Insert floral wire through hole in bottom of one pot and up through the hole in the second pot. Repeat for third pot.

3. Using pliers, twist wire end together, securing pots.

4. Prepare floral Styrofoam. Refer to Technique 4, Step 2a on page 43.

5. Glue one piece of floral Styrofoam to inside bottom of each pot.

6. Position and glue silk roses onto floral Styrofoam in one pot as desired.

7. Position and glue pepper-berry sprays around silk roses as desired.

8. In second pot, position and glue cherry sprays onto floral Styrofoam near rim of pot.

9. Position pear in center of cherry sprays as desired. *Note: Floral picks come with wire attached to one end so that they can be secured to arrangement if pick is not long enough to reach the floral Styrofoam. Also, wire can be added for stem length. Refer to Technique 2, Step 5j–l on page 38.*

10. In remaining pot, position and glue daisy onto floral Styrofoam as desired. Position and glue greenery in and around daisy as desired.

Wooden-petal Floral Variation: The wooden-petal flowers in the arrangement featured above have been placed into a clay pot embellished with seashells. This eye-catching arrangement will seemingly last forever.

project
18

How do I arrange only a few flowers?

What You Need to Get Started:

Florals
Individual blooms

Supplies
Appropriately
sized containers

Sometimes less is more. A few perfect flowers can make a dramatic impact when displayed effectively. Even a single blossom, ever so powerful in its loneness, can become a striking floral masterpiece.

As featured above, the flower floats alone and isolated in a jar. Fill the jar half way with water and top it off with a lid to complete the arrangement. So simple, this particular floral arrangement works inside at the dinner table as well as outside on a porch.

Floating gracefully in their personal wading pool, a threesome of magnolias dances in the springtime sunshine. This floral arrangement, as featured above, can be duplicated by removing the stems from the flowers, keeping the top two or three leaves intact. Then position magnolias in a pretty bowl filled with water.

The prettiest or most interesting part of a container or vase is sometimes the rim, which is oftentimes hidden by the floral arrangement itself. Try placing a solitary blooming flower into that specific vase and show off that rim.

Section 4: *art of flowers*

Flowers, regardless of whether they are fresh, silk, dried, grown in the garden, purchased, or created by hand, are an art in and of themselves. They are also a means by which to create pieces that give a message without words, share the beauty of nature without a walk in the garden, or lift your spirit without any help at all.

The photographs of these designs in Section 4 are meant to inspire you to create something truly beautiful from that which surrounds you every day. Use flowers to sit on your table, hang on your wall, or adorn your front door. Add mementos, keepsakes, or souvenirs to give additional meanings. Use, add, and create the unexpected—it is so easy to do. The basic techniques are easily learned and mastered and all else that is needed is a good idea or a little imagination.

Glossary
This book has called for the flower names that are the most commonly used.

Fresh Florals

Anthurium,
aka: Painter's Palette
- Various colors
- No scent
- 7–14 days as a cut flower

Baby's Breath,
aka: Gypsophila
- White; pink
- Distinctive scent
- 10–14 days as a cut flower

Bird of Paradise,
aka: Strelitzia
- Bright orange and purple blooms
- No scent
- 7–14 days as a cut flower

Calycina
- White
- No scent
- 7–14 days as a cut flower

Carnation,
aka: Dianthus
- Various colors
- Distinctive scent
- 7–10 days as a cut flower
- Delicate stem

Chrysanthemum
- Various colors
- Distinctive scent
- 7–10 days as a cut flower

Cushion Pompon
- Various colors
- Distinctive scent
- 7–14 days as a cut flower

Daisy, aka: Bellis
- Various colors
- Distinctive scent
- 7–14 days as a cut flower

Feverfew,
aka: Chrysanthemum Parthenium
- White
- Distinctive scent
- 7–10 days as a cut flower

Forsythia
- Yellow
- Slight scent
- 7–10 as a cut flower
- Delicate stem

Gerbera Daisy
- Various colors
- Slight scent
- 7–10 as a cut flower
- Delicate stem

Godetia
- Various colors
- Slight scent
- 7–10 days as a cut flower

Heather, aka: Erica
- Lavender, rose, white
- Distinctive scent
- 10–14 days as a cut flower

Hydrangea
- Various colors
- No scent
- 7 days as a cut flower

Hypericum
- Reddish-orange
- Slight scent
- 7 days as a cut flower

Iris
- Various colors
- Slight scent
- 7–10 days as a cut flower
- Delicate stem

Isralia Ruscus, aka: Butcher's Broom
- Green
- No scent
- 14 days as cut foliage

Ivy, aka: Hedera
- Solid green; variegated green
- No scent
- 2–4 days as cut foliage

Larkspur, aka: Delphinium Consolida
- Various colors
- Slight scent
- 7–10 days as a cut flower

Leather Fern
- Green
- No scent
- 10–14 days as cut foliage

Lemon Leaves
- Green
- No scent
- 14 days as cut foliage

Leucadendron, aka: Silver Bush
- Dk. red
- No scent
- 10–14 days as cut foliage

Mini Carnation, aka: Dianthus
- Various colors
- Distinctive scent
- 7-10 days as a cut flower
- Delicate stem

Mini Pittosporum
- Green; variegated green
- No scent
- 10–14 days as cut foliage

Oncidium, aka: Dancing Lady Orchid
- Greenish-yellow; rose-lilac
- No scent
- 10–14 days as a cut flower

Peony
- Cream; dk. maroon; pink ; red; white
- No scent
- 7 days as a cut flower

Peppercorn
- Green
- No scent
- 7 days as cut foliage

Pittosporum
- Green; variegated green
- No scent
- 7 days as cut foliage

Protea, aka: Proteus
- Various colors
- No scent
- 7 days as a cut flower

Rose
- Various colors
- Strong scent
- 7 days as a cut flower

*Snapdragon,
aka: Antirrhinum*
- Various colors
- No scent
- 7–10 days as a cut flower

*Sprengeri Fern,
aka: Asparagus Fern*
- Green
- No scent
- 5–10 days as cut foliage

Stargazer Lily
- Pink; white
- Strong scent
- 7–10 days as a cut flower

*Statice,
aka: Limonium Sinuatum*
- Pink; purple; white
- No scent
- 10–14 days as a cut flower

Stock, aka: Matthiola
- Cream; pink; white
- Strong scent
- 7–10 days as a cut flower

*Sunflower,
aka: Helianthus*
- Orange; rust; yellow
- No scent
- 7–10 days as a cut flower

*Sweet Pea,
aka: Lathyrus*
- Various colors
- Strong scent
- 7–10 days as a cut flower
- Poisonous

Sweetheart Rose
- Various colors
- Strong scent
- 7–10 days as a cut flower

Tulip, aka: Tulipa
- Various colors
- No scent
- 7–10 days as a cut flower

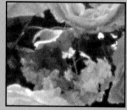

Viburnum
- White
- Distinctive scent
- 7–10 days as a cut flower

Viking Pompon
- Yellow
- Distinctive scent
- 7–10 days as a cut flower

*Waxflower,
aka: Stephanotis*
- Pink; white
- Slight scent
- 5–10 days as a cut flower

Dried Florals

*Allium,
aka: Onion Head*

Eucalyptus

Honeysuckle Vines,
aka: Lonicera

Lavender,
aka: Lavandula

Lotus, aka: Nelumbo

Myrtle, aka: Myrtus

Nigella Pods,
aka: Love-in-a-mist

Nuts

Papaver Giganthus

Pepper Berries

Plumosus

Sheet Moss

Spanish Moss

Thika Pods

Rosebuds

Metric equivalency chart

mm-millimetres cm-centimetres
inches to millimetres and centimetres

inches	mm	cm	inches	cm	inches	cm
⅛	3	0.3	9	22.9	30	76.2
¼	6	0.6	10	25.4	31	78.7
⅜	10	1.0	11	27.9	32	81.3
½	13	1.3	12	30.5	33	83.8
⅝	16	1.6	13	33.0	34	86.4
¾	19	1.9	14	35.6	35	88.9
⅞	22	2.2	15	38.1	36	91.4
1	25	2.5	16	40.6	37	94.0
1¼	32	3.2	17	43.2	38	96.5
1½	38	3.8	18	45.7	39	99.1
1¾	44	4.4	19	48.3	40	101.6
2	51	5.1	20	50.8	41	104.1
2½	64	6.4	21	53.3	42	106.7
3	76	7.6	22	55.9	43	109.2
3½	89	8.9	23	58.4	44	111.8
4	102	10.2	24	61.0	45	114.3
4½	114	11.4	25	63.5	46	116.8
5	127	12.7	26	66.0	47	119.4
6	152	15.2	27	68.6	48	121.9
7	178	17.8	28	71.1	49	124.5
8	203	20.3	29	73.7	50	127.0

yards to metres

yards	metres	yards	metres	yards	metres	yards	metres	yards	metres
⅛	0.11	2⅛	1.94	4⅛	3.77	6⅛	5.60	8⅛	7.43
¼	0.23	2¼	2.06	4¼	3.89	6¼	5.72	8¼	7.54
⅜	0.34	2⅜	2.17	4⅜	4.00	6⅜	5.83	8⅜	7.66
½	0.46	2½	2.29	4½	4.11	6½	5.94	8½	7.77
⅝	0.57	2⅝	2.40	4⅝	4.23	6⅝	6.06	8⅝	7.89
¾	0.69	2¾	2.51	4¾	4.34	6¾	6.17	8¾	8.00
⅞	0.80	2⅞	2.63	4⅞	4.46	6⅞	6.29	8⅞	8.12
1	0.91	3	2.74	5	4.57	7	6.40	9	8.23
1⅛	1.03	3⅛	2.86	5⅛	4.69	7⅛	6.52	9⅛	8.34
1¼	1.14	3¼	2.97	5¼	4.80	7¼	6.63	9¼	8.46
1⅜	1.26	3⅜	3.09	5⅜	4.91	7⅜	6.74	9⅜	8.57
1½	1.37	3½	3.20	5½	5.03	7½	6.86	9½	8.69
1⅝	1.49	3⅝	3.31	5⅝	5.14	7⅝	6.97	9⅝	8.80
1¾	1.60	3¾	3.43	5¾	5.26	7¾	7.09	9¾	8.92
1⅞	1.71	3⅞	3.54	5⅞	5.37	7⅞	7.20	9⅞	9.03

Index

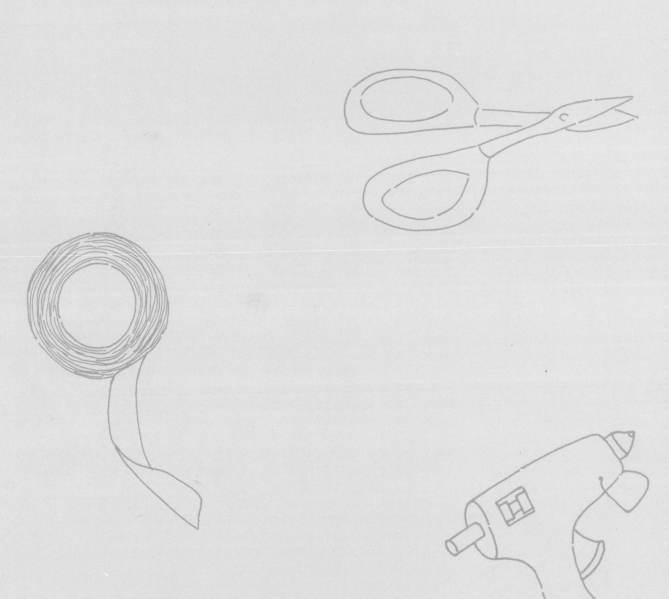